Reflection

Volume 2

By, Piree Rozier

I dedicate this book to Tariq and Taryn.

Table of Contents

DAD 1

ANGER MANAGEMENT 4

Workforce 8

Poemtry 12

Wake Me 15

It's So Cool to Be Black 17

Moral Value 21

Loop 24

Directors Cut 26

Desktop Computer 29

Relationships 31

Two dimensional 33

Apologetic 1.0 36

We vs They 39

-Trix 41

Numbers Game 43

Out-sane 45

Auntie 47

The Self 49

S T R U C T U R E 51

Life Cycle 54

No Consequence 56

A n t e n n a 60

Engineering 64

P O S S I B I L I T Y 68

Societal Reflection 70

Fighting Words 73

Instrucciones 76

DAD

I'm afraid to fail

but I'm proud to stand up and take my position

who am I kidding

I'm irresponsible and immature with no money

who's gonna raise these children?

Changing diapers ain't that hard

preparing bottles, sink baths, rocking to sleep

that's my full-time job

Teaching how to with no prob

Get down from there! don't do that! you better stop!

REFLECTION

My initial reaction to fatherhood was fear. I knew I was good with children as far as babysitting and playing goes. When you're responsible for another human that can't do for themselves, that's a different level of responsibility. I have insecurities about "knowing how to be a man", since my father wasn't there for me and my stepdad and I didn't spend much time together. I've had examples of what manhood is supposed to be from watching my stepdad, uncles, television shows and men at church. When my son was born I was trying not to panic in the delivery room. The nurse asked if I was excited, I very calmly said yes and proceeded to cut the umbilical cord.

My son changed me a lot but the more things change the more they stay the same. Meaning I was still drinking heavily, we were out and about every weekend or hosting our own house parties. Good or bad my baby boy was with us almost every step of the way. He was an easy-going baby, he didn't cry unless he was hungry or needed his diaper changed. When he was sleepy he would put his pacifier in his mouth, lay down and go to sleep, baby cool breeze indeed.

When my daughter was born we thought we had this parenting thing downloaded. She changed our perspective immediately. From day one my daughter would cry if my wife wasn't holding her, people always thought we spoiled her but she was born that way. When I held her at the hospital, she would cry if I wasn't singing and walking around so I did a lot of singing. She was a very demanding baby, with a healthy set of lungs. My daughter is also a picky eater. When we gave her mixed veggies she would actually isolate what she didn't want to one side of her mouth and eat what she did want on the other side. I thought it was amazing and that she was part squirrel or something but she likes what she likes.

Today we feel as though we have partially survived parenthood thus far. My son is in high school and my daughter is on her way to middle school. I've made LOTS of mistakes as a young and older parent but it's all a learning process. Hopefully these experiences will make me a wise and patient Grandfather a long, long time from now.

ANGER MANAGEMENT

Ten, nine, eight,

fuck that shit

it won't amount to much

when my mind is programmed for violence

seven, six, five,

who let the demons out?

I control my atmosphere

the cure is your demise

four, three, two,

almost at peace

lying to myself

playing make believe

never made it, guess I lost count...

REFLECTION

This is a mockery of anger management counseling, which I have been a member of more than once. Did it work, nope but it gave me an idea of which direction not to go in. I think meditation, exercise, playing in the sand, walking on the beach, painting and gardening are ideal. My anger issues began at a young age, mostly because my father wasn't there for me. He would occasionally take me to get a haircut and take me to see my grandparents. My only memory of his parents is they would always give me money from their big jars of coins. My interactions with them were minimal because we didn't see each other much. I always felt a void and pain from that but like most children I didn't know how to express it. I was silly, happy go lucky and didn't take much of anything seriously, laughter was my tears of a clown.

As a child, my parents took us to visit a pediatric therapist but I would get angry when asked questions. I told my Mother I didn't want to go back because I didn't want to talk to them. She didn't force the issue and I never returned. A couple of years later I was caught stealing a pellet gun from a big-name store. I was placed on probation. One of the conditions was that I complete anger management because I tried to fight the security guard to get away. I don't recall but I guess I was given a mental evaluation of some sort. This time around I answered questions, completed assignments, participated in exercises in a group setting. Needless to say, it didn't calm me down but it did teach me how to hide my anger very well. As a teen my Youth Pastor told me that when you allow people to make you angry they're controlling you like a puppet on a string.

Years later, in my early twenties I was drinking and partying all the time. I started out as a happy drunk but that slowly changed into something ugly.

There was a situation between myself and a cop regarding

a noise complaint for loud music. It was the after party for my son's baby shower in 2006. We were at our friend's apartment, when our friends neighbor who also happens to be the leasing agent comes outside. She didn't get along with my friends' girlfriend at all, they had a couple of arguments prior to. So, when she came outside to complain to them it did not end well and she said that she was calling the police. The police arrived while I was inside sitting down. I could've remained inside my friend's apartment but my anger said go confront the police and I said okay. Once outside I walked past my friends and began my bullshit. After words were exchanged with attitude from both sides, we were told to pack up the DJ equipment. As I went to turn around the cop said, "hurry up boy", with 'that' tone, you know the one. Lit the match, BOOM! I called him everything but a child of God, he didn't like that of course. He flickered his flashlight by my side to distract me and said he's going for something. As I looked to my side he ran up and grabbed me in an attempt to arrest me. A scuffle ensued at first but I stopped resisting and he pinned me against the building. I asked, "What the fuck are you doing?" He said, "You're going to jail for obstruction of justice", and proceeded to handcuff me.

    Right after that my pregnant girlfriend said something to the cop protesting the arrest. He turned and walked towards her in an aggressive manner. I walked up behind him to protect her from whatever I thought he was about to do. Before he could get to her I shouted, don't put your hands on her (or something like that) his attention turned back to me and he leg swept me a couple of times. As I was going down I turned my body and fell on my back. The handcuffs dug into my wrist, OUCH. I yelled at him to pick me up because of the cuffs, he did and took me to the car. As we were headed to the police station I cursed him out and pleaded my case. He acted nonchalant at first, he understood my point but wouldn't admit he was wrong.

    I asked him how would he feel if someone called him a boy in a racist, disrespectful tone at his sons' baby shower. He was silent but I knew the wheels were turning in his mind. On the way to the jail he stopped at a church to meet his partner to 'talk.' I couldn't hear what was said but I was thinking they were plotting to do me bodily harm or worse. Come to find out they were putting a story together. He returned to the car and we headed to the Cobb County jail. I didn't know the extent of my injuries until I sat down to be booked.

When I looked at my wrist and my knee, I cursed at the cop some more and demanded he take the handcuffs off, which he did. After having to bond out, go to several court dates, etc. my anger had cost me a great deal. Honestly everything was cool between my friends and the cops until I went to confront them. I was also facing a felony because the cop lied and said I head butted him. It was a blatant lie because he didn't say that on the scene and his partner was there and didn't bother to intervene. I used my "get out of jail free card" and pleaded no lo-contender, which I still regret to this day. I wanted to fight that bastard til the end because he lied on me and it shows on my record like maybe he did, maybe he didn't.

My lawyer also told me to pursue a civil suit and to contact the NAACP. There's a two-year statute of limitations and I let it lapse, DAMN. The last thing my lawyer said to me was "See Tavarus not all of us are evil", I thought that was interesting, was he talking about white people or lawyers, or both. You live a lot, you'll definitely learn a lot. There are plenty of other stories but I'll save those for later. Experience has been one of my best teachers and anger is a sneaky enemy. I'm not completely against counseling. I agree with whatever works for the greater good, plus it's better than jail and lawyer fees... NAMASTE

Workforce

I'm tired

not complaining, just bitching

sleepy from life's duties

fuck a 15-minute break

We deserve a 15-year hiatus

A 15-week vacay

in 15 different places

Never planned on getting older

but no wishes of being Peter Pan

done for the night

tapping out and clocking in

fighting 40 hours

weekend warriors

planting seeds

from which we may never smell the flowers

Why?

children, family, luxury, greed

wants, expensive taste, bad habits, needs

I propose implementing mandatory nap time

furthermore

coloring books, playgrounds and adult snack time

until it's I started my own biz, I quit time

pursuing the elusive dollar sign

street scholar

blue- or white-collar crime

who run it

not me, not yet

rat race face ass, on your mark, get set

capitalism with no criticism

I need the dollars

dollars is what I fiend for

join the system

trading time

for currency

trading energy

for currency

after I get enough

they'll decrease the value

certainly

oh well, I'll stay my course

overpower, overcome,

outwork the workforce

REFLECTION

I never planned on joining the workforce and I don't believe in the "American Dream." A wise person once said if you fail to plan then you plan to fail. Which is what I did, I've worked for numerous companies because I didn't want to be there in the first place. I went about starting my own business the wrong way a countless number of times. I was too busy partying and bullshitting mostly. There's nothing wrong with working for someone else, it definitely provided for my family at the time. I've also learned a lot about business operations, finances, logistics, etc. while employed. Every situation is a classroom, in hindsight putting myself in uncomfortable places prepared me for my ultimate goal. Besides that, I wasn't ready to operate a business back then.

I will say if you have a dream, goal or just an idea in mind, pursue it at all costs. Don't wait for the perfect time or for the stars to align. Minimizing regrets is much better than having to live with them roaming in your head. We are our own worst enemy so get the fuck out of your way and make it happen, whatever it may be.

Poemtry

Permission to take flight

comes with no wings or lessons

asking, begging, slows progression

lacking, loathing, procrastination my confession

inspired by what

acquired superficial, materialistic,

low frequency, non-vibration,

bunch of buy me now

pay me later, crumb saver aspirations

fuck you lay me, with no consideration

I can't get involved

I'm too busy looking for God outside of myself

down a dead-end avenue

blessed to be breathing they told me, yet I can't find the gratitude

that ain't the half of it

thoughts on papyrus is ancient art

Been there, came here, and I'll be around when the buck stops injecting soul, fiending for more, I'm becoming cyclops

can't close my third eye nor moisturize it with eye drops

open interpretation, of my undercover overestimation

I love myself

I love y'all too

REFLECTION

Just rambling off my random yet focused outlook of different areas in life at the time. Things change, myself included so my views here might be different somewhere down the line. I'm a poet and an unintentional riddle writer so sometimes you have to unwrap what I'm conveying. I love myself and I love y'all too.

Wake Me

When I tried to sleep

Nina Simone woke me up

Malcolm & Muhammad woke me up

James Baldwin woke me up

and when I tried to shut my eyes

Carter G. Woodson woke me up

Dr. John Henrik Clarke woke me up

Eldridge Cleaver said wassup

Bunchy Carter lifted me up

When I was tired and tried to lay down

Huey P. spoke me up

Martin King raised me up

Fred Hampton blazed me up

REFLECTION

These are more than names, the inspiration behind the person is enough to revive my motivation. Different energies provide different benefits. I appreciate the ancestors listed and unlisted for the wisdom, guidance and courage to be who they are... We all have work to do.

It's So Cool to Be Black

It's so cool to be black

I like big butts and I cannot lie

turns out jealousy and envy creates

multitudes of wanna be's

big booty with skinny thighs (?)

It's so cool to be black

until the police have questions

fist bumps don't exist

pound in the lesson

It's so cool to be black

misappropriating creativity

stole the drip

wrote your name on it

with no validity

It's so cool to be black

even black people join the wagon

dat way, keep that same energy, ya know trappin trappin

It's so cool to be black

we create dress codes

just so

these other companies can disrespect

us into not fucking with their logos

It's so cool to be black

until the judge bang the gavel

slapped wrist, don't exist

got time plus time

concentration camp cattle

It's so cool to be black

until that gangsta shit

becomes your reality

triple O.G., active 21 savagery

It's so cool to be black

everybody wanna say the n-word

nigga, you say it I'll kill ya

the irony only seems absurd

It's so cool to be black

out living stereotypes

now pass my fried chicken

and watermelon delight

It's so cool to be black

I can teach you

melanin is, what melanin does

genes of isis

I'm the plug

c o o l

REFLECTION

Well.... not only have all of our creations been stolen, copied and envied forever. Most times we get no credit and other times we're dismissed as if we never did anything productive in society at all. I don't feel the need to explain the obvious any further here. I need the education system to teach more of our rich history before and after slavery. But not much is gained by asking, maybe I'll publish a book about it or use one by J.A. Rogers and push to include it in the school system. Better yet the more definitive answer is to start my own school.

Moral Value

Loyalty is on sale,

coupons accepted

Integrity can be bought and sold

the market has reached an all-time low

Dignity will be purchased

for cents on the dollar

No returns even with a receipt

Mr. Honesty is advertising deceit

The want ad is looking for your soul

state your price, some are willing to pay ten-fold

Shame was mislabeled and placed on the top shelf

It's hard to reach, who can help

I'm at the cash register

two cents short from completing my purchase

My opinion is cheap

show me your values, money is worthless

REFLECTION

What does face value mean anymore, it means nothing to me. I'm not really surprised by anything or anyone anymore. Living has made me this way. Optimism is a luxury I can't afford. I still use the cliché, hope for the best but expect the worst to safeguard myself. Never judge a book by its cover boy's and girl's people will surprise and trick you.

Loop

I'm not feeling well

Well what I'm feeling is not my usual

Usually, I'm optimistic

it came and went

which brought me back to the same sentence

I'm not feeling great

Great, here we go again...

REFLECTION

Exactly how I was feeling at the time. It came and went as usual. Having mental health issues is a battle fought against internal opposition.

Directors Cut

Another mass shooting added to the mountain of bullets

Unanswered questions, what could make a man point a weapon with no aim in sight

was he triggered to pull it

In the grand scheme of things your life becomes checkers

Crowned king and moved reckless

Viewing himself victorious by removing pieces, becoming the collector

News flash, headlines, breaking story in endless circulation

What's real

statement or question

Maybe the Dems & Pubs are the old Crips & Bloods

Maybe the story they're stretching

Will be used to choose your selection

Complete control under the guise of protection

Spin the story, lone wolf

bullied youth, retaliation afoot

sympathize, loving son of a saint

you view him as a murderer

We'll tell you what he ain't

Spin the story

taxpayers paid for the show

give it to 'em

trial run, anticipate reactions,

hypothesis

jury of your parents,

the leniency is apparent

Spin the story

dizziness, attention deficit

they'll forget after the next blast

propaganda machine & legislation

business as usual

long live the ruling class

... and scene

REFLECTION

It's no secret that the government, CIA, FBI and other three letter television channels, organizations, etc. have been using media to further their objectives and training exercises. Thing is, legislation was passed that made it legal to lie to the people and it's barely hidden. The masses of us just go along with the propaganda machine for a number of reasons. Crisis actors, staged events, etc. are in abundance so much that I don't know what to believe sometimes.

With this poem I'm not exposing anything because it's public information. Just my insight on the times, I don't know who the director is of course but he or she is like the Wizard of Oz calling the shots. The media helps control the narrative and smooth everything over. If race is involved the story receives plenty of attention and is sensationalized to divide and conquer. If the offender is caucasian their identity is sometimes hidden and their painted in a positive manner. When the person is melanated they were born a criminal and deserved it because they stole a candy bar in second grade.

Racism white supremacist ideology is at play in all functions of life. At this point it's the normalized standard, most of us don't even notice the blatant hypocrisy of it all. This fake world of superiority was created long ago and needs to be constantly combated and eventually destroyed. Some people have a hard time even admitting that such a thing exists but denial will not make it go away. As long as we continue to fight against each other over petty differences and falling for the division tactics we'll never come together and fight against what we agree needs to be obliterated. This division was socially engineered, if people come together and go against the tyranny they won't be able to stop us.

... and the show goes on, take your seats

Desktop Computer

Reconfigured my main frame & saved it to a floppy disc

Zeros & ones, 10's & hunduns

how do we exist

Ran low on megabytes, that's when I pondered a dirt nap

No fairy tales read between the spine,

recognize

real rap

Press the space bar to create distances

among these instances

The arts I seek to master and still retain my apprenticeship

Control alternates, deleting backspaces

Press forward and F everyone

We return the same as we enter

Leave your prints when you run

REFLECTION

I took this from another poem because the two parts didn't make sense together. This is just a little wordplay using computer terms. I just left it as is so I wouldn't start writing anything just to fill it in. I got bars fool.

Relationships

Beauty is her game

I'm on controller one

I'd rather lose to her

Game over we can try again

I thought love was everything

Turns out it's a minute slice

of the many demands in life

Just like that it can all slip away

Active energy, catch a feeling

but don't let it corrupt judgment

Cool heads prevail in the conflict

Let us allow us to be happy

REFLECTION

All relationships are complicated and I don't want to talk about it.

Two dimensional

Another rapper reported dead, phenomenon

lifestyle or scripted reality

All I see is people in costumes

acting out characters, com-icon

Festivities taking place is it awards time or Ramadan

Another entertainer reported dead, surprising

The worlds a stage, make up, lighting, disguising

New scheme, pick a character and start franchising

identity crisis advertising

Lying pays the bills

Another scandal reported, distractions

underhanded government, what really happened

abundance of campaign funds, pocket change

hatred being projected, misguided aim

Lying increases the kills

Another …

REFLECTION

The entertainment industry is huge, influential and almost impossible to ignore. Following other people's lives, lies and drama can be a waste of time. Filtering through the bullshit of whether or not someone is authentic is exhausting. I guess it's all entertainment right or wrong, fiction or truth. Tune in and be careful, attention is an addictive drug and some will do anything to get it.

Apologetic 1.0

Tears of a sideshow Bob

Cries unanswered

You've really done it this time

Only this episode you've managed to push away

Disregard and damage the woman that loves you

Man's man more like a fool's fool

What's your thought process

I need progress

Walking forward looking over my shoulder

what's the past?

Insignificant my ass, learn from last week

Do you know I love you?

Verbs & actions

weights on a balance

I can show you but my mind and movement don't match

Reality needs a surface scratch

Dunce caps or face slaps

I'm your blackberry

I deserve a ton of tears

More importantly I deserve someone like myself

Taste of my own medicinal purpose,

selfish self

Careless actions as though

I'm willing to lose our foundation

Quit playing

Be the man you are

For her first, for your children, for your sanity

Chaotic man, gone mad

I will live up to my title

Husband, lover, dad

Speed bumps don't go on forever

and there's often a back street

Map your course before elsewhere avenue dead ends to divorce

eyes don't rain when my heart pours

my apologies

truly, sincerely yours

REFLECTION

As previously stated, relationships can be complicated. Marriage is complicated, especially if it involves me. I'm not the easiest person to please. I'm not the best communicator because I don't feel the need to explain myself and at times tell anyone what I'm about to do. I feel like I'm asking my wife for permission on a decision I've already made. Although, I get the reasoning I'm not good at it...

Arrogance?

Narcissism?

Pride?

Probably all three, work in progress, yes. I've completed the first step to resolving this problem. Putting it into action is not easy for me because my mind works a certain way sometimes. Compromising is not a strong suite of mine either. Overcoming views and attitudes towards marriage can be easy when put into perspective. My wife is more important to me than my pride. My family is more important to me than my arrogance. The narcissist has to die because I don't benefit from it but it will be a slow death.

We vs They

THEY murdered another one of us

WE changed our conditioning,

response and positioning

THEY lied again, pulling puppet strings, hiding the hand

WE did our own investigating

forget patiently waiting

THEY fear our rise

WE plot their demise

THEY seek to further destroy what we've built

WE seek to build anyway

THEY copy everything we do

WE keep giving everything

who are THEY?

more importantly, who are WE?

REFLECTION

WHO ARE WE?

Know thyself, is an old Afrikan Proverb. I apply it to my life and say it to my children. We need a new direction to take us into a prosperous future.

-Trix

How can I escape the great illusion?

There has to be something, somewhere, someone has the solution

Or am I creating the past and the future

Unplug

REFLECTION

Maat-trix, Matrix, Illusions, Arythmetic, Deja vu, Premonitions...

I don't believe in coincidences, I don't believe in any one thing.

Numbers Game

1 life to live

66 books within

0 fucks to give

7 deadly sins

2 too many

5 human senses

3rd rock from the glow

4th quarter, 4th & inches

8 wonders

9 ether

10 commands

masses of believers

1 life to give

REFLECTION

I was just having fun with numbers, pick it apart.

Out-sane

I'm not losing this time

I have decided to forego normality

You've drawn the line

you've caused my slip-on sanity

Who's falling with me

Who chooses to break the pattern?

Is it Santa, Satan or Saturn

Someone's not telling me something

REFLECTION

We will never know what's going on everywhere and with everything. There are so many sectors in control of different aspects of our society, how will we ever decipher the truth from the lies. You can't beat them, join them doesn't apply here. Knowing is half the battle and it can be a burden; the unknown may be a misunderstood gift. Either way life goes on, right. I try to enjoy the wonderful joys of life while I'm here and loosely focus on things outside of my control.

Auntie

2 aunties passed, reminisce over you

darkness all around and I'm comfortable

37 years in, time is still a trick

I want it all

2 aunties still with us

why do we exist

digesting reality is hard to stomach

chewed up, spit out, societies recipe makes me vomit

refrain

from depression, grief, anger & pain

pictures, videos I obtain

the memories remain

… Auntie

REFLECTION

We all have to live with regrets and not talking to my Aunties more is on my list. I feel like I didn't know enough about them but I do remember some of the things they told me. I used to be a social butterfly and would prank call friends and family. Sometimes I would just call in general to talk. Now I think about reaching out but I put it off and it never happens. I'm antisocial now for some reason and I wish I could get back to the social person I used to be. I've always liked looking at pictures and videos of family known and unknown. I have a collection of memories that I keep to remember us by. Although, I don't call like I used to I think about my family, extended family and friends all the time and I love y'all. I have the videos and pictures to prove it

Auntie Retta

Auntie Jan

The Self

Just jumped over a hurdle

then realized

the biggest one was getting over myself

the mission is to work on the self

if willing then we're able to do things ourselves

selfish & selfless

different jars collecting coins on the shelf

which gets the payment

keeping it all for myself

statement...

choices, I don't care enough

do it yourself

REFLECTION

Search within to find yourself and keep moving. When people would say "I need to find myself", it never made sense to me. You're not lost, what do you mean find yourself, I didn't understand at all. Now I do and I didn't like everything I found about myself. Dealing with and accepting yourself is a part of growing up, I had to figure that out as well. I can be selfless and selfish, in this world I lean more to what's considered selfish. Unfortunately, nice and selfless people are consistently taken advantage of.

STRUCTURE

Parade was rained out

structured upbringing

no learning just programmed thinking

habitual happenstances

patterned thought patterns

I know exactly what you're thinking

demolition man engages

flip the switch

self-hatred propaganda

will damage ya

conquest of division

created leaders and heroes

covers all the bases

halt progression at all costs

improve the conviction rate in all cases

you are not a slave

more like prisoner of warfare

under the guise of citizenship

maritime law, ucc1 game

left to figure it out

game is to be sold

but hide it right under their nose

you are a terrorist if you won't

lay down and accept the treatment

it's the law

I just wrote it

today and tomorrow

America

hysteria

REFLECTION

These words describe our controlled society under the guise of structure. Is structure needed, yes but to what extent. Being raised in a structured household benefited me greatly. Outside of home not so much, only because I'm a rebel looking for any cause. I understand the structure with school, work, leisure activities, etc. What I don't care for is personal choice not being an option when it comes to school, vaccines, food, religion etc. We're almost herded in a certain direction because of outdated standards and beliefs. When this pattern of thinking is taught at a young age some of us grow up thinking in the mindset of someone else. I wrote this with a movie titled Demolition Man in mind, we rented it from Blockbuster (yes Blockbuster) long ago. The demolition man was programmed to carry out someone's plans and he didn't realize it for a long time. The same way movies, music and everything we download to our brains can affect our behaviors and thoughts.

Predictable programmed behavior, continuous control, let it go.

In all factions of life, I think we should question everything to decide whether we still agree or not. That would definitely put everything into perspective and possibly lead to an independent thought process. Maybe some of us are comfortable with the structure after questioning it. Maybe some of us are comfortable realizing the structure and not questioning anything.

Life Cycle

As a child life is simple

As a teen the future is bright

As an adult the struggle is real

REFLECTION

Going backwards is not an option yet so we have to deal with 'it', whatever that may be at times. I only think I want to be a kid or teenager again. If I went back there, I'd be ready to get back to adulthood. Being content where you are is difficult when in the middle of turmoil but that's what makes reaching the outcome so great.

"The grass can be green on both sides if you water that shit, you can't wait on the rain."

-Me

No Consequence

Who made it okay for me to be gunned down?

overkill, cop used more than twelve rounds

motor skills? skin pigment? a strange sound?

heaven knows, no well wishers

just hells hounds, wanting me hell bound

the finish line was home but I missed it by more than a stretch

legs and feet don't move fast enough when chased by death...

it seems

the judicial system had it out for me

the legislative branch wrote the route for me

the executive plan stood on my neck undoubtedly

Why was I here in the first place?

my experience must've been the same as those from yester years

conjured energy, pressured peers

low confidence festered fears

I'm not asking for help

I think my two feet work just fine

I was born on a thin line

puppet master pulling strings unraveling twine

Who made it okay for me to be gunned down?

overkill, cops used more than fifty rounds

sagging pants? dark hoodie? hat pulled down?

Either way I fit the description

no mob just a lynching

suspect, no loss of job nor pension

my family thrown into another dimension

where do we go from here?

rhetorical, theoretical, factual

all in one question

guilty by complexion was the lesson

finale, closed casket, at the trial subtle confessions

Who made it okay for me to be gunned down?

Overkill, cops prejudged me before they fired any rounds

thug? menace to society? felon with a mean frown?

Either way no trial, just a gunshot and a body left to die on the ground

I get blamed and framed on the evening broadcast

"Only if he complied"

"Stop resisting"

"I repeated the command, he wasn't listening"

"I thought it was a weapon, he kept insisting"

Who made it okay for me to be gunned down?

Who made it okay?

Who made it?

Not me!

REFLECTION

This one speaks for itself

Antenna

Connections

no Wi-Fi involved

Reflections

crimes unsolved

Selections

choices made no option to pause

Protection

various weapons

I'm gonna get you sucka

I'm gonna scar you all

Blessings

sacrifices, thrice times life

Who do you call?

Religion, division

Crusader, missions

Accomplished deceit

wash, rinse, repeat

This land is my land

no melody, no preach

No assistance, just leach

Mama told me a lot of things

Tomorrow came and it sunk in

Fortune tellin'

Propelled my mind into the deep end

Theory, I think not

Let it simmer

longer than dinner in the crock pot

Feast

Thank you, Mama

Managing

to manifest

manna

Through magical connections

I AM still here

REFLECTION

What is an antenna? It's a signal puller. I was given lots of great advice and suggestions over the years. I never really listened. It made good sense but at the time I couldn't put it to good use because I didn't know how, I had my own agenda. I'm the antenna in this scheme of words. I'm picking up strong signals from various people (different channels). The problem is the picture wasn't clear yet. As the years went on my antenna grew stronger and I picked up on the signals (messages) from the past and from the present. The picture became clearer and clearer to the point where the image is clear on the screen (my mind) with no static. Some of y'all are probably thinking what is an antenna? I'm an 80's baby so do your google search and find out. In the beginning I'm speaking about aspects of myself and society with no details because I can't make sense of it yet. My antennas signal is basically weak and the picture is scrambled. I'm not seeing things clearly or thinking things through. I'm trying to figure out life, myself and society while operating on a low frequency.

Experience teaches a lot, mistakes will be made again and again and again. The thing is, as long as your trying to do better aka raising your vibrations you'll get where you were meant to be.

Engineering

I've been looking for a motive,

found it

but reasonable doubt isn't within reach

so, I wait,

practice after preach

not guilty through caged free speech

I guess,

due process showed my obsession

slowly revealed my thoughts,

confessions

over time track record clean,

progression

don't judge a book by its cover,

the lesson

turnover in your grave

bedtime, can't sleep

flip the mattress

spring me free

a man's gotta do

what his plans say

follow through

demons, all of em'

72

legions

given asylum

protect me too

evaluations, no fees

just meds and a peaceful room,

doctors

mental reproach

help them fix me

you know assisting

I'm on the rebound

points given as further proof,

all better now

so, they think

I think, I hit em' with everything

except the kitchen faucet

play the game to WIN

after you 'momentarily' lost it

YOU ARE NOT MY JUDGE!

REFLECTION

I never liked the board game monopoly.

POSSIBILITY

Miracles

wins from a two-time loser

it's possible

spirituals

books broken down to fractions, evolving reaper

it's all possible

unity

one accord, mass movement, exodus

it's still possible

REFLECTION

Possibilities are endless even when options are limited, never give up.

Societal Reflection

Victim of society

Vanity for notoriety

The way I see it

Even the truth gonna lie to me

Even the proof won't justify me

Oddly enough, the who, the what

still don't mean much

bang the gavel, liberty is blind

so, things will never look up

my signs, my march won't amount to much

I'll burn this bitch down

that's my crutch

When I need food, medicine, supplies

it's ashes and dust

My anger is unfocused

My target eludes my grasp

Nobody taught me economics, sociology or warfare

So, in my ignorance my fight cannot outlast

Do I blame....

Or impregnate change

Give birth to,

what I think must,

bring death to,

those that brought death to us

ASSIMILATE

REFLECTION

Some of my poems are similar in thought and subject. Mainly because the same issues exist and have yet to be resolved. I tend to dwell on things although most things seem to be out of my control. We all can play an intricate part in finding solutions. Agreeing on a solution or path is a task in itself. Many have tried different methods and here we are... What's next?

Fighting Words

Kill ignorance

bash it's head in with a thick book

knock jealousy the fuck out

stomp every inch of envy

with a foot

choke doubt

I shot the tariffs

but the Prezi pocketed hatred

to implore southern border order

while pinching criticism on its many faces

to the victor goes the spoils

while we punched the time clock

pushed past misconceptions

& mind blocks

insurrection stabs crime stop

fight for your country

double entendre

kick you off the property

that I stole

handcuff freedom

hold the constitution hostage

high ransom

execution style murder the answers

and purposely burn temper tantrums

fists up

silence of the anthem

going down swingin'

liberation sure is beautiful

death sure is beautiful

REFLECTION

Words have power and can bruise without contact. I'm sure someone has said something to you that has stuck with you for years. These mostly violent action words fulfill my angry thoughts and ideas. I'm angry about the things mentioned in this poem because I feel as though I don't have the power to change them. I tend to focus on things that I have no control over, which gives that thing power over me. If I were to focus on what's right in front of me the other things outside of my reach would probably become less important. Maybe I would have the patience and energy to create realistic answers. Everyone has problems but some things we take on and create problems for ourselves. These verbs are my outlet and starting point of letting go of what I allow to control me.

Instrucciones

Turn off your tv

turn on your awareness

unplug your PlayStation

be the controller of your destiny

shutdown the laptop

find your type

delete the app

apply your skills

REFLECTION

There's nothing wrong with technology, I love it. It benefits us greatly but as with everything there are downfalls. Radiation exposure, child labor & slave mining, deteriorated eyesight and attention span deficits are far too common. Research where the cobalt for your cellphone comes from. Look into how often we are exposed to radiation in our day to day, etc.

Use this to find your way.

- Dad

Thank you for joining me. I don't typically tell anyone much of anything about my personal life or share pictures of my children. I have grown to accept how therapeutic it is to talk about internal issues, trauma and troubles.

I love myself and I love y'all too.

Also, on Amazon,

Artistic Reflection Volume 1

SHORT POEMS

You should never kick a man when he's down

I've been stomped out

& checked in

chumped off

& stepped on

it's hard to shake the regret

destiny is calling, press 1 to accept

insult or impress

ravage or relinquish

salvage or repeat sequence

control your breathing

stop thinking

close your eyes

grand delusions from being sleep deprived

no worries, the world is in your palm

just concentrate on being cool, calm

I won't apologize for being better than you

Psychotic episode going over the 30 minute time slot

My reality is unreal

I can't figure it all out on the spot

I need time here

I need a nap and a plane ride

I need assistance

I need to speak to the manager

Help me get out of my own way

But not today

Reruns

Set in the sands of time

These are not just words on paper

Used to roam streets like a vagabond

Lately I've been the co-creator

But not in your context

Open that box and watch nothing jump out

Cuz everything inside is dead from being mislead into thinking that was the route,

Or route (root)

Stupid is, as dumb me down does to a sculpted nincompoop

9 lives of a cat don't mean much if death comes in threes

Climb up to escape danger, falling flat when they shake the trees

That ain't deep,

I'm shallow,

as in ankle deep, low tide, sand castles

I graduated after school with no tassel

Aborted the high road with no hassle

I use words to express myself

I use actions to help myself

Who knew werds were magic

Who knew…

Made in the USA
Columbia, SC
06 January 2025